Destination Detectives

United Kingdom

North
America

Europe

UNITED
KINGDOM

Asia

Africa

South
America

Australasia

Rob Bowden

Raintree

www.raintreepublishers.co.uk
Visit our website to find out more information about **Raintree** books.

To order:
☎ Phone 44 (0) 1865 888112
🖹 Send a fax to 44 (0) 1865 314091
🖥 Visit the Raintree Bookshop at **www.raintreepublishers.co.uk** to browse our catalogue and order online.

Produced for Raintree by
White-Thomson Publishing Ltd,
Bridgewater Business Centre,
210 High Street, Lewes, BN7 2NH

First published in Great Britain by Raintree,
Halley Court, Jordan Hill, Oxford OX2 8EJ,
Part of Harcourt Education.
Raintree is a registered trademark of
Harcourt Education Ltd.

© Harcourt Education Ltd 2006
The moral right of the proprietor has been asserted.

Editorial: Sonya Newland, Melanie Waldron,
and Lucy Beevor
Design: Clare Nicholas
Picture Research: Amy Sparks
Production: Chloe Bloom

Originated by Modern Age
Printed and bound in China
By South China Printing Company

10 digit ISBN 1406203076
13 digit ISBN 9781406203073
10 9 8 7 6 5 4 3 2 1
11 10 09 08 07 06

British Library Cataloguing in Publication Data
Bowden, Rob
  United Kingdom. - (Destination detectives)
  1.Great Britain - Geography - Juvenile literature 2.Great
Britain - Social life and customs - 21st century - Juvenile
literature 3.Great Britain - Civilization - Juvenile
literature
  I.Title
  941'.086

Acknowledgements
Rob Bowden pp. 6 (Chris Fairclough Worldwide),
7 (Chris Fairclough Worldwide), 8-9 (Chris Fairclough
Worldwide), 9 (Chris Fairclough Worldwide), 12-13
(Chris Fairclough Worldwide), 19, 20r, 21, 25, 26-27, 33,
34, 37 (Chris Fairclough Worldwide), 42 (Chris Fairclough
Worldwide); Corbis pp. 15 (Ashley Cooper); Getty Images
pp. 16-17 (Matt Cardy), 23 (Scott Barbour), 26, 43;
Photolibrary pp. 4 (Photolibrary.Com, Australia), 5l (Jon
Arnold Images), 10 (The Travel Library Limited), 11
(Photolibrary.Com), 13 (Photolibrary.Com), 22 (Robin
Smith), 24t (Index Stock Imagery), 26, 27 (Tony Bomford),
31 (Foodpix), 38 (Niall Benvie), 40 (Ruth Brown), 43;
Topfoto pp. 5t, 14-15 (Gordon Nicholson/Spectrum Colour
Library), 24b (ESC), 30 (Gordon Davis), 35 (Photonews
Service Ltd Old Bailey), 36 (WDS), 38-39 (Brandt); WTPix
pp. 5m, 5b, 17, 18-19, 20l, 28-29, 32, 40-41

Cover photograph of Big Ben and the Houses of Parliament
reproduced with permission of Photolibrary/Purestock.

Every effort has been made to contact copyright
holders of any material reproduced in this book.
Any omissions will be rectified in subsequent
printings if notice is given to the publishers.

The paper used to print this book comes from
sustainable resources.

Disclaimer
All the Internet addresses (URLs) given in this book were
valid at the time of going to press. However, due to the
dynamic nature of the Internet, some addresses may have
changed or ceased to exist since publication. While the
author and publishers regret any inconvenience this may
cause readers, no responsibility for any such changes can be
accepted by either the author or the publishers.

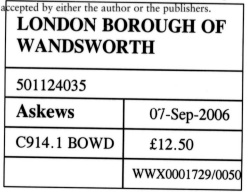

Contents

Any words appearing in the text in bold, **like this,** are explained in the glossary. You can also look out for them in the Word Bank box at the bottom of each page.

Where in the world?

Notting Hill

Notting Hill is the biggest street carnival in Europe. The first carnival was held in 1965 as a celebration of London's **multicultural** population. More than one million people gather in this small part of north London every August to watch dancing, drummers, and carnival floats.

As you step outside your hotel you hear the most incredible noises coming from a nearby street. There are drums and whistles, trumpets and guitars, and the sound of voices. You follow the noise, and as you round a corner you see hundreds of people, of all different backgrounds. They are dancing and waving, and some are dressed in amazing costumes. It is a carnival – but where are you? Where in the world has people from so many different backgrounds?

During the Notting Hill Carnival, people parade through the streets along a 5-kilometre (3-mile) route, dancing and wearing colourful costumes.
▼

4   **WORD BANK**   **multicultural** society that has people from several different countries or cultures

Just as you are trying to work it out, you notice a bright-red double-decker bus. On the back it has an advert for a new musical, which reads "Now showing in London's West End". So you are in London, the capital city of the United Kingdom (UK). A voice nearby calls to you: "Come and join in the fun – everyone is welcome at the Notting Hill Carnival."

The Carnival is a celebration of the many different cultures that live side by side in London.

Find out later...

Why are these people chasing a ball of cheese?

What are these famous landmarks?

How is the United Kingdom reducing road traffic?

The United Kingdom at a glance

SIZE:
244,101 square kilometres (94,248 square miles)

OFFICIAL NAME:
United Kingdom of Great Britain and Northern Ireland

CAPITAL:
London

POPULATION:
60.4 million

TYPE OF GOVERNMENT:
Constitutional monarchy

OFFICIAL LANGUAGE:
English

CURRENCY:
British pound (£)

A few streets away from the carnival you find a café. Inside, on the wall, is a large map of the United Kingdom, covered with postcards and notes that have been sent in by other travellers. There is also a book all about the United Kingdom. What a great place to look for clues about what this country is like!

The United Kingdom is a **union** of four countries – England, Wales, Scotland, and Northern Ireland. England and Wales formed a union in 1536, and they were joined by Scotland in 1707. Ireland became part of the union in 1801, but in 1921, the southern part of Ireland was declared independent. Only Northern Ireland remained part of the United Kingdom.

Countries of the United Kingdom

Country	Area (sq. km/sq. miles)	Population (2001 census)
England	130,410/50,351	49.1 million
Scotland	78,789/30,421	5.1 million
Wales	20,758/8,015	2.9 million
N. Ireland	14,144/5,461	1.7 million

The Giant's Causeway, on the coast of Northern Ireland, is made up of thousands of columns of a rock called basalt. They were created during a volcanic eruption 60 million years ago.

WORD BANK constitutional monarchy form of government where there is a king or queen and a parliament

Scotland and Wales are the least populated and most mountainous regions of the United Kingdom.

The United Kingdom has a long and varied coastline that stretches for a total of 12,429 kilometres (7,723 miles).

Orkney Islands

Shetland Islands

Hebrides

NORTH ATLANTIC OCEAN

Scottish Highlands

SCOTLAND

Edinburgh

Glasgow

NORTH SEA

NORTHERN IRELAND

Belfast

Newcastle

The United Kingdom has many historic cities, including London, Oxford, Edinburgh, and York.

ENGLAND

York

Leeds

IRISH SEA

Liverpool

Manchester

Sheffield

Lincoln

IRELAND

Nottingham

Wales has its own language, and signs are written in both Welsh and English.

WALES

River Severn

Birmingham

Coventry

Colchester

Oxford

London

Cardiff

Cotswolds

River Thames

Bath

Southampton

Brighton

N
W E
S

Plymouth

0   200 km
0   100 miles

English Channel

FRANCE

CHANNEL ISLANDS

An historic land

Sun temple

Each year on Midsummer's Day (21 June), **druids** gather at Stonehenge to celebrate the dawn. On this day, as the sun rises, it is lined up exactly with the stones. This has led many people to believe that Stonehenge was built by ancient people as a temple to worship the sun.

People have lived in the United Kingdom for thousands of years. To discover more about the country's history, you decide to visit the ancient site of Stonehenge. This is a circle of standing stones near Salisbury, in southern England. No one knows why the stones were put there. It might have been a place of worship, an **astronomical** calculator, or perhaps a palace. The oldest parts of Stonehenge were built over 5,000 years ago. Some of the stones are up to 9 metres (30 feet) high and weigh around 50 tonnes (49 tons).

Stonehenge is arranged as four circles, one within the other. It is surrounded by a wide ditch.

▼

Fast fact
Stonehenge is not the oldest stone circle in the United Kingdom. The stone circle at Avebury in Wiltshire is even older and larger than Stonehenge, although not so well-preserved.

WORD BANK   AD number of years from the birth of Jesus Christ in the Christian calendar
astronomical relating to the stars and planets

Roman Britain

In AD 43, Roman armies from Europe landed at Rochester in southern England, and the Romans became rulers of large parts of the United Kingdom for almost 400 years. They built many important cities, including York, Lincoln, Bath, Colchester, and London. The Romans also built some of the earliest roads across England, such as the Fosse Way. The route of this can still be seen today.

➤ Hadrian's Wall marks the boundary that existed between England and Scotland during Roman times.

Hadrian's Wall

In around AD 122, the Roman Emperor Hadrian ordered his soldiers to build a fortified wall to protect Roman Britain from the tribes of **Barbarians** that lived in Scotland. The wall took six years to build, and was 118 kilometres (73 miles) long from coast to coast. Parts of the wall are still visible today.

Barbarians ancient people known for aggressive warfare
druids people who worship the forces of nature

Great inventors

The Industrial Revolution was a time of many new inventions. The first steam-driven machine was built by the Englishman Thomas Savery in 1698 to pump water out of flooded coalmines. By 1765, the Scottish inventor James Watt had invented steam engines to work machinery in mills. The Englishman Richard Trevithick built the first steam train in 1804.

A revolution begins

Although the Romans have left many ancient remains, you want to find out about the more recent history of the United Kingdom. You decide to follow the old Roman roads, the Fosse Way and Watling Street, until you reach an area known as the Black Country near Birmingham.

The Black Country was at the heart of the **Industrial Revolution** in the United Kingdom during the 18th century. Around the year 1700, people discovered how to make iron, a strong metal that could be used for buildings and machinery. Ironbridge, which spans a **gorge** over the River Severn, is a lasting symbol of this important time.

Ironbridge in Shropshire was the first bridge made of iron in Europe. It was built by Abraham Darby, and opened on New Year's Day in 1781.

WORD BANK

empire number of countries ruled by one nation
gorge deep natural gap in the landscape, normally formed by a river

All change

Iron-making led to the invention of many new machines – and the use of steam instead of humans or animals to power these machines. Hundreds of factories opened, and **ports** and railways were built to transport all the goods that were being made. Many of the United Kingdom's largest cities began to grow at this time, including Liverpool, Manchester, Birmingham, Glasgow, and Belfast. The Industrial Revolution helped the United Kingdom become the world's wealthiest and most powerful country at the time.

British lords and ladies visit the palace of an Indian prince at the beginning of the 20th century.

Age of Empire

In the 17th century, the United Kingdom started to conquer other parts of the world so it could improve its trade with other countries. With all the money created by the Industrial Revolution, this foreign **empire** grew dramatically, and by 1900 the United Kingdom ruled almost a quarter of the world's land and people.

Industrial Revolution period of rapid improvements in industry and technology
port place where boats and ships load and unload their cargo or passengers

11

Century of change

Home of the Titanic

The Harland and Wolff shipyard in Belfast is one of the United Kingdom's last remaining shipyards. The ship *Titanic* was built here in 1911, and was the world's largest ocean liner, at 268 metres (883 feet) long and 28.2 metres (93 feet) wide. It weighed around 39,000 tonnes (38,400 tons). The *Titanic* sank on its first voyage, on 15 April 1912.

As you explore the Black Country, you notice that many of the industrial centres are now museums. There is not much left of the industries that made the United Kingdom, and this part of it in particular, so powerful. So what happened to change the country's fortunes?

The United Kingdom at war

In the first half of the 20th century, the United Kingdom fought two world wars in Europe, in 1914–1918 and again in 1939–1945. Over 1.5 million people from the United Kingdom were killed and many cities were badly damaged by bombing in World War II. The wars also cost a lot of money and industries suffered badly, as they did in many countries at this time.

During World War II, the city of Coventry was badly bombed. Today, the new cathedral (on the left) stands next to the ruins of the old one (on the right). ➤

WORD BANK   import buy goods such as food and machinery from another country

Industrial decline

In the 1950s and 1960s, things began to improve, and many new jobs were created. However, in the 1970s, UK industries began to decline once again. Other countries began to make products for less money, and so the United Kingdom **imported** goods instead of making them. Coalmines, **textile** mills, shipyards, steelworks, and vehicle manufacturers closed down, and thousands of jobs were lost.

A woman works on a train during World War II.

Women at work

To replace the men who went off to fight during World War II, women took on jobs in factories and on farms. For many women this was the first time they had ever worked. Before this, most women stayed at home to look after their families. Today, women make up 44 percent of all UK workers.

textiles material made by weaving or knitting

You are here!

• Manchester

Modern Manchester

To see how the changes of the last century have affected the United Kingdom today, you head to Manchester, one of the United Kingdom's greatest industrial cities.

One of the first things you notice about Manchester is that many of the old industrial buildings are still there. Most of them have been turned into offices, shops, and even homes. There are many new parts of the city, too, with enormous shopping and entertainment centres. These are the new industries of the United Kingdom, known as "service industries". They provide services such as banking, insurance, entertainment, retail, information, and travel.

The Internet age

E-commerce is business that uses the Internet, and it is growing quickly in the United Kingdom. Books, music, holidays, and even groceries can now be bought on the Internet and the goods delivered to your door. E-commerce is providing thousands of new jobs for people in the United Kingdom.

Ethnic groups in the United Kingdom

White – 92.1 percent
Black – 2.0 percent
Asian – 4.0 percent
Mixed – 1.2 percent
Other – 0.7 percent

The Urbis Centre in Manchester is just one example of the modern architecture that is replacing the old buildings. It is a museum that explores **urban** culture and city life.

WORD BANK   colonies parts of the world that are ruled by another country

Building boom

Elsewhere in Manchester, you see some old tower blocks and houses being pulled down. These were once the homes of the people who worked in the factories. When the factories closed, many people found new jobs in other parts of the city, and moved away. You see a sign showing a picture of the new housing, shops, and offices that will be built to replace the cramped old housing. All this demolition and rebuilding has made construction one of the United Kingdom's most important industries. The building boom is happening in cities all over the country.

Young Muslim boys outside a mosque in Leeds. 2.7 percent of the UK population is Muslim.

The world in the United Kingdom

Before the 1950s, there were very few Black or Asian people living in the United Kingdom. After the war, the country invited people from its **colonies** to come to live and work there. Tens of thousands came from the Caribbean, Africa, and South Asia. This is one of the reasons why the United Kingdom is so **multicultural** today.

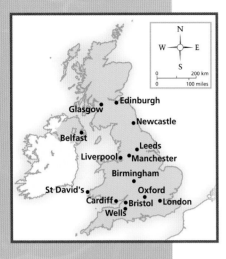

Manchester is one of the United Kingdom's largest cities, and it grew because of its industries. Other cities in the United Kingdom have grown for different reasons, although not all are as big as Manchester.

- London is the capital, and the biggest city in the United Kingdom, located on the River Thames. It has been an important trade centre since Roman times.

- Oxford is a centre of learning, and is well-known for its university, which is one of the oldest in the world.

- Edinburgh is the Scottish capital, and has one of the best-preserved castles in the United Kingdom. It hosts the Edinburgh Festival – the largest arts festival in the world.

Small cities

In the United Kingdom, a city is somewhere that has been given the title by the king or queen. Wells, in Somerset, southern England, has a population of just 10,000, and is the smallest city in England. The smallest city in the United Kingdom is St David's in Wales, with just 1,600 people. It is named after the patron saint of Wales, St David, who was born there in AD 520.

People line the streets in Edinburgh's Royal Mile during the famous festival.

WORD BANK City of London one of the oldest parts of London

- Birmingham is the United Kingdom's second-largest city and was once its most important industrial city. Today it is one of the main centres for shopping, entertainment, exhibitions, and conferences.

- Cardiff is the Welsh capital, and was once one of the United Kingdom's busiest **ports**. Today it is an important business centre and has one of the UK's best sports stadiums.

- Belfast is the capital of Northern Ireland and an important industrial port and shipyard.

▲ New buildings being constructed at the docks in Cardiff.

City identities

People from some cities in the United Kingdom have been given nicknames. Mancunians are from Manchester and Scousers from Liverpool. Geordies come from Newcastle Upon Tyne, Brummies from Birmingham, and Cockneys from London. To be a true Cockney, you have to have been born within hearing distance of the bells of St Mary Le Bow, a church in the **City of London**.

United Kingdom's largest cities

City	Population
London	7,188,000
Birmingham	2,272,000
Manchester	2,252,000
Leeds	1,433,000
Newcastle	1,026,000
Liverpool	951,000
Glasgow	579,000
Edinburgh	449,000
Bristol	405,000
Cardiff	305,000
Belfast	277,000

17

You are here!

London•

London life

London is by far the biggest city in the United Kingdom, so you decide to head back to the capital to find out a bit more about life in the cities.

Like all British cities and towns, London has a mixture of houses. There are some very wealthy areas, with expensive town houses, but close by there are run-down and overcrowded **estates**. The cost of housing in London is especially high because it is the capital city and there is a shortage of homes. New housing is being built on old industrial land, and many old **warehouses** have been turned into luxury flats.

The Docklands

Canary Wharf is one of the newest parts of London. It was built on part of London's **derelict** old docks. It is a major new business centre, and is connected to the rest of the city by its own railway system. Among its many new buildings is Canada Tower, the tallest building in the United Kingdom, at 237 metres (778 feet) high.

Canary Wharf, in East London, is a thriving modern business and residential centre.

18 **WORD BANK** commute travel into a city from another area to get to work
derelict run-down and abandoned

Commuting

Because housing is expensive, many people choose to live on the outskirts of the city where it is cheaper. These people **commute** to the city centre to work. This means that many British towns and cities are spreading outwards. Every day, millions of people make their way into London and other cities to go to work. They travel mostly by car, by train, or by bus. At the beginning and end of the working day, city transport systems can grind to a halt with so many people on the move.

A display in Trafalgar Square in London forms part of the campaign for the city to host the 2012 Olympics.

Olympic boost

In 2005, London won a competition to host the Olympic Games in 2012. The games will be based in a run-down and poor area of east London called the Lower Lea Valley. The games will help to revive this part of London with new transport, housing, and other facilities.

estate area of housing
warehouse large building used to store goods

Fun in London

All across London you notice posters advertising many different events. There are festivals and exhibitions, museums and galleries, and hundreds of shows, including theatre, ballet, opera, cinema, and music concerts. This is one of the benefits of living in a large town or city – there is always so much to do! As you continue your investigations, you make some notes about the benefits and problems of living in the city.

The Manchester tram system has reduced road traffic by two million car journeys a year.

London's West End is packed with theatres showing world-famous plays and musicals.

On the tram

Several cities in the United Kingdom have introduced **trams** to try to keep people moving in the busy centres, and to reduce road traffic and pollution. The Manchester tram system has 37 kilometres (23 miles) of track, 32 trams, and carries 52,000 passengers every day.

WORD BANK   tram type of train that runs on rails through city streets

Benefits

- Lots of job opportunities.
- Many different transport choices (including bus, train, underground).
- A chance to meet people from many different cultures.
- Many restaurants, theatres, and museums to enjoy.
- Good shopping facilities, with many specialist shops and markets.

Problems

- Traffic congestion on the roads and air pollution from exhausts.
- Crowded transport systems at busy times.
- High cost of living (things are very expensive).
- Some very poor areas where people struggle to get by.
- In parts of some cities, there can be a lot of crime.

The Tube

London's underground railway system, known as the Tube, has 274 stations and 408 kilometres (253 miles) of track. Three million people travel by Tube every day.

Taste the world

Cities in the United Kingdom offer a choice of food from around the world. In London there are hundreds of restaurants, where you can try food from countries including Italy, Spain, France, China, India, Japan, Morocco, Vietnam, Thailand, and Cuba.

Several cities, including London, have their own "Chinatown" – streets full of Chinese restaurants, where Chinese culture is celebrated.

➤

Education

Cities and towns have many opportunities for learning, and most universities and colleges are in **urban** areas. To find out more, you leave London and head to the United Kingdom's most famous centre of learning – Oxford.

The University of Oxford began teaching in the 12th century, and is the world's oldest English-language university. It is also one of the best in the world. There are 125 universities in the United Kingdom, with 2.25 million students. About 43 percent of people between the ages of 17 and 30 study at university.

The boat race

Every year, students from Oxford University take on students from Cambridge University (the second-oldest in the United Kingdom) in a rowing race. It takes place every spring on the River Thames. The first Oxford and Cambridge boat race took place in 1829. Today, around 250,000 people gather on the banks of the Thames to watch the two universities battle it out on the water.

Christ Church College in Oxford was established in 1546. Thirteen British prime ministers have attended this college since it opened.

WORD BANK compulsory something that the law says you must do

Schools

School is **compulsory** in the United Kingdom for all children aged four to sixteen years. There are three main stages of schooling in the United Kingdom:

- Primary school – all children from the age of four until eleven.
- Secondary school – all children from the age of eleven until sixteen. Examinations called GCSEs are taken at the end of this period.
- Upper secondary school – for children aged sixteen to eighteen, who study for advanced level (A-level) examinations or Highers in Scotland, which are needed to go to university and some colleges.

As well as schools and universities, there are hundreds of colleges in the United Kingdom. These teach practical skills to train students for particular jobs, such as plumbing, bricklaying, hairdressing, catering, and various skills in healthcare.

Learning for fun

Many people in the United Kingdom choose to learn for fun. There are lots of courses available at colleges, from photography or flower-arranging to cake design or flamenco dancing! Most people study these for personal interest, but some go on to turn them into a job. People often study these subjects as evening classes.

In secondary schools, there are usually around 30 students per class.

Life in the countryside

On a roll!

The United Kingdom has several unusual countryside traditions. One of these takes place at Cooper's Hill in Gloucestershire. People run down a very steep hill, chasing after a large circular cheese. The winner is the first to reach the bottom – the cheese is their prize! The tradition of cheese-rolling dates back to Roman times.

Oxford is surrounded by some of the most beautiful villages in the United Kingdom, in an area known as the Cotswolds. This is a good place to find out what life is like in the countryside.

A traditional bakery in a Cotswold village. Stores like this often have more than one use. ▼

Thousands of people gather to watch the annual cheese-rolling event at Cooper's Hill. ▼

Before the **Industrial Revolution,** most people in the United Kingdom lived in small villages such as those in the Cotswolds. Of course, villages today have cars, electricity, telephones, and other modern conveniences. Many, however, are still made up of a cluster of houses around a village centre, with a church, school, store, and perhaps a market or village green. Today these villages are popular with visitors wishing to escape city life.

WORD BANK plague highly infectious disease
remote far away from other places or people

Remote villages

In **remote** areas, many village facilities have closed because people have moved to the cities. This can make life difficult in some **rural** areas, which are many miles from the nearest shop or post office. Some villages in Wales and Scotland are especially remote. In some places, services are combined to try to improve life for the people there. There are over 200 Postbus services, for example, which combine delivering mail with a local bus service.

The Plague Village

Eyam in Derbyshire is one of the United Kingdom's most famous villages. In 1665, a tailor called George Viccars brought cloth back from London that contained fleas infected with the **plague**. Within a year, the disease had killed more than 375 people – half the population of the village.

PLAGUE COTTAGE

Mary Hadfield, formerly Cooper, lived here with her two sons, Edward and Jonathan, her new husband, Alexander Hadfield and an employed hand George Viccars.

George Viccars, the first plague victim, died on 7th September 1665
Edward Cooper, aged 4 died on the 22nd September 1665
Jonathan Cooper, aged 12, died on the 2nd October 1665
Alexander Hadfield died on the 3rd August 1666
Mary alone survived, but lost 19 relatives.

The house that George Viccars lived in – the man who brought the plague to the village of Eyam.

rural relating to the countryside

Farming

The countryside is about much more than attractive villages. Farming is an important industry in the United Kingdom, producing food for local needs and for **export**.

Farming varies greatly around the United Kingdom. The flat, level lands of East Anglia are ideal for large cereal and vegetable farms using giant farm machinery. In lowland areas with gentle hills, there is a mixture of crop and livestock farming. In the more hilly regions of Wales, northern England, and Scotland, livestock farming (especially of sheep) is more common. In southern England, the warmer **climate** allows fruit such as apples, pears, and grapes to grow.

Countryside jobs

There are many traditional jobs still found in the countryside:

- Farrier – someone who makes and fits horseshoes.
- Gillie – an attendant who cares for hunting and fishing grounds in Scotland.
- Crofter – someone who runs a small farm (croft) in Scotland.

A farrier fits a horseshoe in Devon, in the south-west United Kingdom.

WORD BANK   climate normal weather conditions of an area

Weather and climate

Farming is dependent on the weather, but the climate in the United Kingdom is generally mild – not too hot or too cold – and with a regular amount of rainfall.

The spring and summer months (March to August) are the warmest months, and the autumn and winter (September to February) are much cooler. Highland areas, and the north and west of the United Kingdom, are generally wetter and cooler than the south and east.
There can be snow in the winter, especially on the higher ground.

Farming in the United Kingdom is largely mechanized today, and huge combine harvesters are used for gathering crops.

Extreme weather

The United Kingdom rarely experiences extreme weather events such as hurricanes or tornadoes, but they do happen. In 1987, a hurricane caused major damage to buildings and woodlands in southern England. In 2005, a tornado destroyed several houses and businesses in Birmingham.

Survival tip

The weather in the United Kingdom can change very quickly, so when you go out, be prepared!

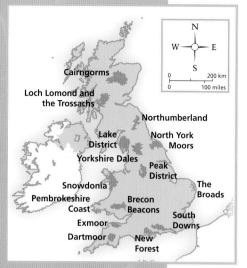

The Scottish Highlands

Parts of the countryside in the United Kingdom are still very **remote** and largely unspoilt by human activity. To discover this wild side of the country, you head to the Highlands of Scotland.

This part of Scotland is one of the last places in the United Kingdom where much of the country's natural wildlife can be seen. The animals you can see here in their natural **habitats** include red deer, seals, whales, dolphins, otters, red squirrels, and golden eagles. The jagged cliff coastline is also home to millions of seabirds, including puffins, which, unusually for birds, nest in burrows.

National parks

The United Kingdom's national parks protect around ten percent of its land area. The first to be established was the Peak District in Derbyshire in 1951. The newest, the New Forest in southern England, was added in March 2005.

The golden eagle is a rare sight in the United Kingdom – there are only around 500 of them left in the Scottish Highlands.

WORD BANK   habitat area where a plant or animal normally lives
heath area of land covered with herbs and shrubs

Other wilderness areas

Other wilderness areas in the United Kingdom include:

- The mountains of Mourne – an area of low-lying mountains in Northern Ireland. The highest peak is Slieve Donard, which is 852 metres (2,796 feet) high.
- Snowdonia – a region of mountains, lakes, and **heath** in Wales. It includes Mount Snowdon, which is 1,085 metres (3,560 feet) high.
- Dartmoor and Exmoor – two areas of **moorland** in south-west England. They are well-known for their beautiful scenery, and are popular with walkers.

Fast fact
The highest mountain in the United Kingdom is Ben Nevis in the Scottish Highlands, at 1,343 metres (4,406 feet) high.

Going wild
National parks and other wilderness areas in the United Kingdom are used by millions of people every year for walking, cycling, horse riding, and more extreme sports. These can include rock climbing, abseiling, canoeing, and canyoning – white-water rafting without a raft!

Crummock Water and Fells forms part of the Lake District in northern England, which was made a national park in 1951.

moorland large area of open land with patches of heath and bogs

Eating & drinking

After the fresh air of the Highlands, you are ready for something to eat. Because the United Kingdom has traded with and ruled over many countries in its long history, much of the food available here has an international flavour. There are still some **regional** specialities, however, including right here in Scotland.

Whisky

Scotland is world famous for a local drink called whisky, made from malted barley. Whisky is stored in wooden barrels for four to twelve years before it is bottled and sold. There are many types of whisky, and some are very expensive. In 2005, a rare 62-year-old bottle of Dalmore whisky sold for £30,000.

Regional favourites

Haggis – A Scottish dish made of a sheep's stomach stuffed with **offal**, onions, oats, **suet**, herbs, and spices, and eaten with bashed neeps (mashed turnip/swede) and chappit tatties (mashed potatoes).

Haggis is sold in shops and served in restaurants all over Scotland.

Black pudding – A dark-coloured sausage popular in northern parts of United Kingdom, made mainly from pigs' blood.

Laver bread – A seaweed and oatmeal cake, eaten as part of a traditional fried breakfast in Wales.

WORD BANK offal an animal's internal organs such as the heart and liver
regional relating to a certain region or area of a country

Champ – A Northern Irish dish, made of potatoes fried in butter with onions and cabbage or leeks.

Barm brack – An Irish sweet bread, made with spices and dried fruit.

Pork pie – Originally from Melton Mowbray in England, this is a pastry case around chopped and spiced pork meat.

Cornish pasty – Folded pastry filled with meat, potatoes, carrots, and other vegetables.

Bakewell pudding – A sweet pastry filled with a mixture of egg, almonds, and sugar on top of strawberry jam. It comes from the town of Bakewell in Derbyshire.

Local markets

One of the best places to try out local food is to visit a farmers' market. These are popular across the United Kingdom and sell many specialities, such as local sausages, cheeses, pies, cakes, and even drinks.

Farmer's markets are the best places to buy fresh food. You can even talk to the people about how they grew, or made, the food.

Fast food

Fast foods like pizzas, burgers, and pre-packaged microwave meals have become very popular in recent years. Because these foods are quite fatty, however, there is also a problem of more and more people in the United Kingdom becoming overweight.

Traditional food

If you don't fancy any of the United Kingdom's local specialities, there are plenty of other foods to choose from. The most famous traditional meal is fish and chips, and there is hardly a town in the country without a fish and chip shop. Roast beef, pork, lamb, or chicken dinners are still popular, especially on Sundays or for special occasions. Shepherd's pie – a layer of minced lamb, onions, and vegetables in gravy, topped with mashed potato – is another popular meal.

Foreign favourite

Indian food is especially popular in the United Kingdom. Manchester has the "Curry Mile", an area with around 50 Indian restaurants in it!

Traditionally, fish and chips were served wrapped in newspaper, and people still enjoy the meal eaten straight from the wrapping.

WORD BANK plantation large area growing a single crop and employing many workers

English tea

People in the United Kingdom love to have a cup of tea, but tea is not grown in the country. Tea was first brought to the United Kingdom from China in 1653, and it quickly became the national drink. A tea trade grew between China and London, with fast-sailing boats called tea-clippers rushing the tea home. In the 19th century, the United Kingdom established its own tea **plantations** in India and Africa, and this is where most tea comes from today.

The *Cutty Sark* is the last surviving tea-clipper in the United Kingdom. It was built in 1869 to bring tea from China.

The legend of Cheddar

Cheddar cheese takes its name from Cheddar **Gorge** and caves in Somerset, south-west England. Local legend says that a milk-maid left a bucket of milk in one of the caves for safekeeping. When she returned some time later, it had turned into a hard and tasty cheese. Cheddar cheese is still produced in Cheddar today.

Having tasted some of its food, you are interested to find out more about the country's culture. A "What's On" guide gives you some clues about other traditional events.

- *Romeo and Juliet* – A new performance of this great play from one of England's most famous writers, William Shakespeare.

- Morris-dancing festival – Morris groups tour the country, celebrating this traditional folk dance that dates back to the 13th century.

Male-voice choirs

Wales is world-famous for its male-voice choirs. Made up entirely of men, these choirs are especially strong in southern Wales, but are found throughout Wales and beyond. They sing powerful songs, many of them in the Welsh language, such as the national anthem *Mae Hen Wlad Fy Nhadau* ("Land of My Fathers").

Morris dancing traditionally celebrated country festivals, such as May Day (1 May).

- London Open Buildings – Visit some of the capital's most incredible buildings in a celebration of the United Kingdom's architecture.

- Sheep-dog trials – Watch in amazement as dogs answer to their master's commands to round up sheep into a pen in the hills of mid-Wales.

- Belfast Music Live – A chance for local musicians to be seen and heard. They could be the next Beatles, Rolling Stones, or Elton John.

- Edinburgh Festival – A celebration of culture in the United Kingdom, with theatre, comedy, music, poetry, and hundreds of acts. This is one of the world's biggest arts festivals.

Festivals

Hundreds of festivals are held every year in the United Kingdom. They range from arts festivals, like the one held in Edinburgh, to pop-music festivals like Glastonbury, where bands play live on stages set up in fields. There are also festivals of film, literature, and other types of music, such as jazz and classical.

Glastonbury is the largest music and performing arts festival in the world. It is held most years on a farm in south-west England.

A mixture of religions

The United Kingdom is a mainly Christian country, and there are hundreds of churches and cathedrals. However, most other world religions are also practised here, especially in the larger cities, where the population is most mixed. Liverpool is a good place to discover these many different religions.

Christianity

The city centre of Liverpool is dominated by its two enormous cathedrals. Liverpool Cathedral is the **Anglican** cathedral, the largest in the United Kingdom and fifth-largest in the world. It took 74 years to build, and was only completed in 1978. Not far away is the Catholic **Metropolitan** Cathedral of Christ the King. It is known for its modern style of architecture.

Islam in the United Kingdom

The first mosque in the United Kingdom, "The Little Mosque", opened in 1889 in a back room of Brougham Terrace in Liverpool. It was started by a local lawyer, who converted to Islam whilst recovering from an illness in Morocco.

Fast fact
The grand organ in Liverpool Cathedral has an incredible 9,765 pipes!

The modern Metropolitan Cathedral in Liverpool can seat 2,300 people.

WORD BANK   Anglican member of the Church of England

All faiths

Elsewhere in Liverpool, there are other places of worship for Jews, Sikhs, Muslims, Buddhists, and others too. Many of the United Kingdom's largest cities have a similar mix of religions, though in general, Wales, Scotland, and Northern Ireland have fewer and smaller non-Christian populations.

A group of young Muslims study their holy book, the Koran. Today there are thought to be 1.6 million Muslims in the United Kingdom.

The monarchy

Queen Elizabeth II is head of the Church of England. She is the latest in a long line of kings and queens, dating back more than one thousand years. The monarch was once the head of the Government. Today, the Prime Minister controls the Government, but the monarch remains an important cultural symbol of the United Kingdom.

Travel & tourism

The National Cycle Network

In 1995 an organization called Sustrans started to build a national cycle network in the United Kingdom. The aim was to encourage people to cycle more for both work and leisure. In 2005, the network celebrated reaching 10,000 miles (16,093 kilometres) of cycle paths.

From Liverpool it is possible to travel almost anywhere in the United Kingdom, but what are the best means of transport available here?

Rail

Liverpool is connected to a national rail network that covers a total distance of 16,814 kilometres (10,448 miles) across England, Wales, and Scotland. Northern Ireland has its own rail network of around 460 kilometres (286 miles).

Roads

The United Kingdom's roads cover a total distance of 392,391 kilometres (243,820 miles) and connect almost every part of the country.

Almost 75 percent of the United Kingdom's population live within 3.2 kilometres (2 miles) of the National Cycle Network.

WORD BANK   terminal place where transport begins and ends its journey

Motorways with up to four lanes of traffic in each direction connect the main population centres, but these make up less than one percent of the United Kingdom's road network.

Ferries

Because it is an island, the United Kingdom has lots of ferry services that connect the mainland with the islands off its coast, as well as running between the islands themselves. For the people who live on the islands off the west coast of Scotland, the ferry services are a lifeline, bringing food, post, doctors, and other necessary supplies. Larger ferries also operate services to neighbouring countries in Europe. Dover, Harwich, Plymouth, and Holyhead are some of the major ferry **terminals**, but there are many others, including Liverpool.

The CalMac ferry provides services between 22 islands off the west coast of Scotland.

Fast fact
Heathrow airport, to the west of London, is the busiest international airport in the world.

Tourist attractions

Some older forms of transport have become popular tourist attractions. Old steam railways that once carried coal or **slate** in Wales, now offer rides to thousands of tourists every year. A network of canals and inland waterways is also popular. But what else attracts tourists in the United Kingdom?

History and landscape

The United Kingdom's long history draws many visitors. They visit historic buildings such as Edinburgh Castle or historic towns and cities like York, with its Roman remains, and Stratford Upon Avon – the home of Shakespeare. There are many famous buildings in London that tourists travel to see, including the Houses of Parliament, Westminster Abbey, and St Paul's Cathedral.

▲ The Eden Project attracts nearly two million visitors a year.

The Eden Project

The world's largest greenhouse – a glass building for growing plants – lies in an old quarry in Cornwall. It is part of the Eden Project, an education centre about plants and **habitats** from around the world. Since it opened in 2001, it has become one of the United Kingdom's top tourist attractions.

WORD BANK   slate grey stone mined to make roof tiles

People also come to enjoy the United Kingdom's beaches, or visit dramatic coastal scenery such as the volcanic pillars of the Giant's Causeway in Northern Ireland.

Museums and galleries

There are hundreds of museums and art galleries across the United Kingdom, from small exhibitions in villages to the national museums and galleries. The most popular are the Tate Modern, the British Museum, the National Gallery, and the Natural History Museum, which are all in London.

Gardens and houses

Many **stately homes** and gardens are open to tourists for some or all of the year. Some of the most popular houses to visit are Chatsworth in Derbyshire and Blenheim near Oxford. Popular gardens include Kew in London and the Botanic gardens of Edinburgh, Belfast, and Glasgow.

The Houses of Parliament and Big Ben (the bell inside the clock tower) are two of London's top tourist attractions. ◄

stately home grand house of important and wealthy families

Stay or go?

From Liverpool you travel to Brighton on the south coast of England. The coast, **pier**, and the South Downs here make Brighton one of the United Kingdom's most popular tourist centres. From here you are just a short train or bus journey from Gatwick or Heathrow airports should you choose to go home. But what if you decide to stay? What is there left to discover?

Island hopping

To the west of Brighton is the Isle of Wight, which is famous for its boat races. Further north, there is the Isle of Man, in the middle of the Irish Sea, where carthorses still pull **trams** along the seafront as they did in the 19th century. Other islands are the Scilly Isles off the south-west coast, and the Shetland and Orkney Islands, north of Scotland. Scotland also has hundreds of smaller islands off its western coast. Located between England and France are the Channel Islands of Jersey and Guernsey.

Curling gold

Curling is one of the United Kingdom's more unusual sports and dates from the 16th century. A curler releases a stone across a sheet of ice towards a target. Other members of the team use brushes to rapidly sweep the ice in front of the stone to help it slide along. In the Winter Olympics of 2002, the Scottish team won the gold medal.

Brighton Pier opened in 1899, and today it attracts over two million visitors a year.

WORD BANK   loch lake or deep narrow inlet from the sea in Scotland

Sport

You could tour the United Kingdom discovering its many different sports, from traditional games like soccer, rugby, cricket, and tennis, to newer sports like surfing, in-line skating, and mountain biking. Attending a big soccer or rugby match with thousands of excited supporters is an experience to remember!

The Needles, off the coast of the Isle of Wight, are a series of chalk rocks. A lighthouse stands on the outermost stack.

▼

Myths and legends

You could spend some time tracking down the myths and legends of the United Kingdom, such as the **Loch** Ness Monster, said to live in Loch Ness in Scotland. Many people come to look for the mysterious beast, but scientists have never found proof of it living there.

pier platform built on stilts that juts into the sea

Find out more

Destination Detectives can find out more about the United Kingdom by using the books and websites listed below.

World Wide Web

If you want to find out more about the United Kingdom, you can search the Internet using keywords such as these:

- United Kingdom
- London
- Scotland
- Wales
- Northern Ireland

You can also find your own keywords by using headings or words from this book. Try using a search directory such as www.google.co.uk.

The British Embassy

The British Embassy in your own country has lots of information about the United Kingdom. You can find out about the different regions, the best times to visit, special events, and all about the culture. In the United Kingdom, this information can be found at: www.fco.gov.uk.

Further reading

Collins Keystart United Kingdom Atlas (Collins, 2006)

Countries of the World: United Kingdom, Rob Bowden (Evans Brothers, 2005)

Nations of the World: United Kingdom, Brian Innes (Raintree, 2004)

The Changing Face of the United Kingdom, Rob Bowden (Hodder Wayland, 2004)

WORD BANK   allies supporters during a time of war

Timeline

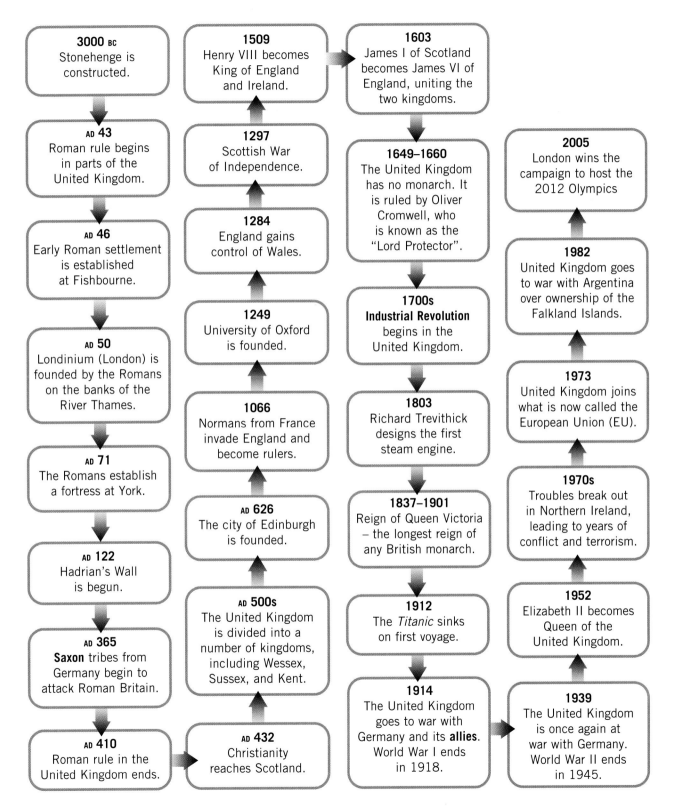

3000 BC
Stonehenge is constructed.

AD 43
Roman rule begins in parts of the United Kingdom.

AD 46
Early Roman settlement is established at Fishbourne.

AD 50
Londinium (London) is founded by the Romans on the banks of the River Thames.

AD 71
The Romans establish a fortress at York.

AD 122
Hadrian's Wall is begun.

AD 365
Saxon tribes from Germany begin to attack Roman Britain.

AD 410
Roman rule in the United Kingdom ends.

AD 432
Christianity reaches Scotland.

AD 500s
The United Kingdom is divided into a number of kingdoms, including Wessex, Sussex, and Kent.

AD 626
The city of Edinburgh is founded.

1066
Normans from France invade England and become rulers.

1249
University of Oxford is founded.

1284
England gains control of Wales.

1297
Scottish War of Independence.

1509
Henry VIII becomes King of England and Ireland.

1603
James I of Scotland becomes James VI of England, uniting the two kingdoms.

1649–1660
The United Kingdom has no monarch. It is ruled by Oliver Cromwell, who is known as the "Lord Protector".

1700s
Industrial Revolution begins in the United Kingdom.

1803
Richard Trevithick designs the first steam engine.

1837–1901
Reign of Queen Victoria – the longest reign of any British monarch.

1912
The *Titanic* sinks on first voyage.

1914
The United Kingdom goes to war with Germany and its **allies**. World War I ends in 1918.

1939
The United Kingdom is once again at war with Germany. World War II ends in 1945.

1952
Elizabeth II becomes Queen of the United Kingdom.

1970s
Troubles break out in Northern Ireland, leading to years of conflict and terrorism.

1973
United Kingdom joins what is now called the European Union (EU).

1982
United Kingdom goes to war with Argentina over ownership of the Falkland Islands.

2005
London wins the campaign to host the 2012 Olympics

Saxon people from West Germany, who arrived in the UK during Roman rule

UK – facts & figures

The flag of the United Kingdom is nicknamed the "Union Jack". The red cross on the blue background, with a white edge, is the cross of St George, the patron saint of England. The diagonal red cross is the cross of St Patrick, the patron saint of Ireland. This sits on the diagonal white cross of St Andrew, the patron saint of Scotland.

People and places

- Population: 60.4 million.
- Life expectancy at birth:
  men – 76 years;
  women – 81 years.
- Highest point: Ben Nevis –
  1,343 metres (4,406 feet).
- Lowest point: The Fens –
  –4 metres (–13 feet).
- Coastline: 12,429 kilometres
  (7,723 miles).

Trade and industry

- Workforce: 29.8 million.
- Unemployment rate:
  4.8 percent.
- Main imports: machinery,
  fuel, food products.
- Main exports: chemicals,
  food products, drinks.

Technology boom

- Telephone lines:
  34.9 million.
- Mobile phones:
  49.7 million.
- Internet country code:
  .uk.
- Internet users:
  25 million.

Glossary

AD number of years from the birth of Jesus Christ in the Christian calendar

allies supporters during a time of war

Anglican member of the Church of England

astronomical relating to the stars and planets

Barbarians ancient people known for aggressive warfare

City of London one of the oldest parts of London

climate normal weather conditions of an area

colonies parts of the world that are ruled by another country

commute travel into a city from another area to get to work

compulsory something that the law says you must do

constitutional monarchy form of government where there is a king or queen and a parliament

derelict run-down and abandoned

druids people who worship the forces of nature

empire number of countries ruled by one nation

estate area of housing

export selling food and products to other countries

fortified protected by forts

gorge deep natural gap in the landscape, normally formed by a river

habitat area where a plant or animal normally lives

heath area of land covered with herbs and shrubs

import buy goods such as food and machinery from another country

Industrial Revolution period of rapid improvements in industry and technology

loch lake or deep narrow inlet from the sea in Scotland

metropolitan urban area, normally including a city and its suburbs

moorland large area of open land with patches of heath and bogs

multicultural society that has people from several different countries or cultures

offal an animal's internal organs such as the heart and liver

pier platform built on stilts that juts into the sea

plague highly infectious disease

plantation large area growing a single crop and employing many workers

port place where boats and ships load and unload their cargo or passengers

regional relating to a certain region or area of a country

remote far away from other places or people

rural relating to the countryside

Saxon people from West Germany who arrived in the United Kingdom during Roman rule

slate grey stone mined to make roof tiles

stately home grand house of important and wealthy families

suet hard white fat from sheep or cattle, used in cooking

terminal place where transport begins and ends its journey

textiles material made by weaving or knitting

tram type of train that runs on rails through city streets

union when countries are joined together politically

urban relating to cities or built-up areas

warehouse large building used to store goods

Index

Titles in the *Destination Detectives* series include:

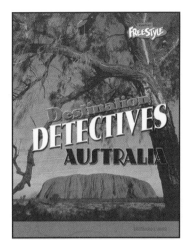

Hardback   1 406 20312 2

Hardback   1 406 20308 4

Hardback   1 406 20306 8

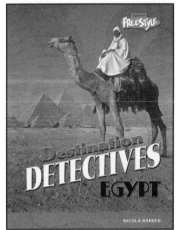

Hardback   1 406 20310 6

Hardback   1 406 20313 0

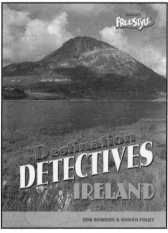

Hardback   1 406 20311 4

Hardback   1 406 20305 X

Hardback   1 406 20307 6

Hardback   1 406 20314 9

Find out about the other titles in this series on our website www.raintreepublishers.co.uk